Roberta Lo

One & one make three

VERITAS

Published 1989 by
Veritas Publications
7-8 Lower Abbey Street
Dublin 1

Original Italian edition published 1986 by
Edizioni Paoline
Via Paolo Ucello 9
20148 Milan

ISBN 1 85390 023 0

Translation: Luke Griffin
Typesetting: Printset & Design Ltd, Dublin
Cover design: Paul McCormack
Cover photograph: Frank Gavin Photography Ltd., Dublin
Printed in the Republic of Ireland by
The Leinster Leader

To my parents

Contents

1982

3 June

It was about that time of the month. On 22 May I was expecting my period... it didn't come. I decided to check.

My own home test was positive. The test at the clinic was also positive. I am pregnant, probably since 2 May, pregnant with a child that I have longed for so much. In the afternoon John came to the clinic to collect me. He read the results of the test from the small sheet of paper and eventually he too was overcome with emotion.

We went to my parents to tell them. My father wept tears of joy, special tears, tears saved up for this very occasion.

I continue to feel a little nausea that seems to date back to the time when I was expecting my period; there is a pain in the pit of my stomach and a strong feeling of tightness in my breasts. Today I phoned Jane, my cousin. She gave me the address of her gynaecologist. He had brought her children and her sister's children into the world. I made an appointment with him for 11 June.

10 June

Who would ever have thought that it was going to be so difficult? There is nothing for it but prayer. But it is the kind of prayer that happens when you really do not know what else there is to do.

This very evening I suddenly began to understand the situation of those sad, cheerless, pregnant women. Women distraught with fear of what is happening within them, happening inevitably, inescapably.

Sarah once said that 'They cannot understand because they have no children...all that we have gone through...all the sacrifices we make.' At the time those sentiments appeared to me to be meaningless. But now I know what she meant and I know that it was true.

Until you have had the experience you cannot understand what it means to feel like this. No woman, no matter how well she has coped, can judge those who are not bearing up too well. Unless you are in the situation you have no idea how difficult it is or how much help you need, how much strength and self-control are required in order to act as others want you to act: a beautiful, calm young mother full of hope while remaining carefree and as interested in sex as you ever were. But if you are in poor health, not as well-balanced as you might be and without love, how easy can it be then?

What do men know of all this? Or even women, what do they know? And those who have been well during their pregnancies, what would they know of how you feel?

Nobody can sit in judgment. I, too have been critical — I must remember this. There ought to be an eleventh commandment: 'Love and respect pregnant women and be charitable towards them at all times'.

Everything is so strange. But this is what I wanted. Only

now can I understand the many women I have examined, without being able really to feel for them. What a lesson for life, there are so many things it will help me understand. That in itself will be a benefit. I am so uncomfortable; I can't see anything clearly.

O Lord, help me! Allow me to live this marvellous and important experience without annoying other people, without, as John says, 'dramatising'. It is not his fault if he has a different role to play and if he fails to understand me: he probably has his own problems, his own crises and upsets and, just as I would like him to understand me, grant that I too may be able to understand his problems.

11 June

I went to the gynaecologist. He believes that I am well. My womb is clearly pregnant but a little bigger because of the amenorrhoea, given that I had early ovulation. Soft and no contractions.

The little lump on my breast which I had noticed at the beginning of my pregnancy and which is now about the size of a cherry, is put down to mastitis; this is frequent in cases like mine. The gynaecologist orders a mammograph. I am to telephone him in a month and arrange to have some tests.

6 July

It probably won't always be like this: I would do anything to make him love you too. But for the moment, little one, I am alone in loving you.

I am looking forward to you being born. Already you are keeping me company. You will not remain with me always. Perhaps you will be close for only a short time and even then against your will, but the very fact that you exist is so important for me.

Even if you never leave me alive you have been with me for three months. Carrying you is really the greatest thing that has happened in my life. The number of things you have already taught me is incredible and I know, if you are born, that you will have many more things to teach me Please be born! My life will have so much more meaning. Just to have given birth to you will represent an enormous victory! I did not believe it would have been like this. And yet I feel so alone in this undertaking. Then again, perhaps it is only right that it should be like this. Perhaps from now on it is nobody else's business but yours and mine.

I have never felt any love like the love I have for you. I made love in order to make you; I eat in order to build you up and make you grow; as far as possible I live my life calmly, in peace and quiet so that even now you should feel happy. My little child, I do not think I could ever love anyone like you, not even if you have a little brother. You are the first. It is with you that I am living through this experience for the first time.

You began your existence with the coming together of a random egg and a stray spermatozoa and you were capable of attaching yourself to my body in order to survive. It is not true to say that children do not ask to be born. Children do not ask us to come together in love because they do not exist at that stage. But once they come into being they have a definite will to exist. I feel it, I feel your will to live; for every day you are with me you make me change so that you will survive until tomorrow. I become calm, wise and loving, and this is because of you; this is your way of protecting your fragility from my carelessness. My nausea is a constant reminder of your presence. You oblige me to take things easy. John doesn't understand us.

I had thought that he would have looked forward to you eagerly; instead he seems to have distanced himself from us. He looks down on us because of our desire for calm; he does not realise that we are right, that this is how we have to live: calmly, thinking only of growing. Everything else is a useless distraction. But when he sees you, he too will understand, and if he does not abandon us he too will learn to live.

18 July

I do not want to talk to him any more about you; it is not worth getting annoyed about it. After a few days during which things seemed to improve to some extent, yesterday and today there was total incomprehension again. He remains aloof — perhaps he does not want you or, perhaps ... he is a mere man.

I know I am doing the right thing for you in avoiding fatigue. Already, even before you are born, you are coming between us. What will it be like when you are born? All I know is that you are there and that I cling to you more than to anything, even more than I do to John, even though I do not like that situation which I would never have believed possible. But that is how things are: at least until you have become more stubborn than he is, I would always choose you. I hope I'll never have to make the choice.

Lord, help me. You always listen to me. Open his mind and heart. Make him understand how much his son and I will need him, how much we need a better him. Let him understand that his son and I are not against him. Let him not be jealous of our son and disparaging of my bulge; may he welcome his son and accept the changes in me; I hope he doesn't stay away from home. Gradually he will enter into harmony with us and all three of us will be together.

25 July

Today was my second visit to the gynaecologist. Again, everything was excellent. He told me to discontinue the vitamins, to carry on with the iron tablets and to begin calcium tablets. The heart became evident. A beat of about 110. A little beauty. It seemed like a little train.

Now John calls you 'baby chuff chuff', 'Poppet'. We didn't know what way to talk about you. 'The baby' seemed so banal and impersonal. Moreover, even if I feel that you are going to be a boy, we still have no idea what we are going to call you. For the moment we have decided to call you 'Poppet'.

30 July

Since you have come along my time is no longer my own, my nights are not my own. I wake punctually at 3.00 and go to the toilet. Tomorrow I will wake because you move. Soon it will be because you cry, because your sleep is disturbed, then afterwards because you are out late at night and then, who knows...?

But I am happy that you are here. I am not and never shall be alone again.

At one time I used to think that I would like to die. But not any more. I cannot want death because that would mean that you would die too. Life is full of promise, of things to do, things to learn and things to teach. I am much calmer now.

I am so happy that you are going to be born. To have reached this stage, this month, is such a joyful satisfaction, such an unbelievable experience.

1 September

I returned home from the country to the city and I began to think of when I would actually be giving birth. I am beginning to be afraid, afraid that something will happen you, afraid for myself, afraid of pain.

How much better I will understand women when this is all over.

The fear is irrational. No one can help. It passes just as quickly as it came about. Perhaps it is because some women have never really had to come to grips with fear that they somehow lose their nerve before and after. One way or another I will have to face up to that moment; time is passing; the baby is growing inside me and the day of birth is approaching. If you are ready you will live through it; if you are not you will suffer through it. Whether you are ready or not it will happen of its own accord. The moment cannot be put back: at a certain point in time the baby wants to come out; the womb begins to contract, it pushes him out even if you are inclined to say — 'no, wait, we will do it tomorrow, we will wait a while!'

The child emerges. You are left stultified. He carries on. He is taken into the hands of strangers. He is no longer you and you are no longer part of him. He has bid you goodbye and laid claim to his own share of life. Already, he desires what you can no longer give him. You are left confused, lost, useless like an empty vessel. You are almost disappointed that he succeeded without wanting to, that while you are overcome with pain, no longer even capable of pushing, at the end you did not even help him. You are afraid of feelings of bitterness towards him because his birth caused you so much pain.

How much more pain will this child cause you! How much pain have you given your own mother? But life is like that. If it is a boy he will never understand you; if it is a girl she will only understand when she herself has this experience. Not before then.

I must never say to my child: 'Look at all the sacrifices I made for you.' The child might perceive this to be a lifelong accusation. This was how I saw things and I never understood what my mother meant when she made that sort of remark; I used to answer: 'Well, who forced you to do it? I didn't ask you to.' I didn't realise then that it is life that asks us to do these things. One doesn't choose all the sacrifices that one makes. My mother didn't throw these things back in my face, she didn't taunt me. She just reminded me and herself of the way things are.

8 September

Yesterday was the beginning of another month. Very sick. Sick stomach and tension. This evening for the first time I am sure I felt you moving.

A veritable storm in the pit of the stomach. Distinct kicks without any rhythm. Then the little chick begins to scratch. More kicks; one here, another there.

The lump on my breast is growing. I must have it seen by an oncologist.

That is all I need: to die from cancer now that I am expecting you.

12 September

The doctor finishes examining me. He looks at me calmly. The word 'benign' encircles the confusion of my thoughts like a rainbow after a storm. I ask him if I will be able to breastfeed you. 'You can do whatever you like — ride a bicycle if you want to.' Thus, with a joke, the tension of the past few days disappears.

15 September

How long does it take to have a baby? When it happens to my friends time seems to fly. Now that it is my own turn I realise that it crawls.

Since coming back to the city at the end of the summer I must admit that I am glad that a considerable amount of time still remains. I am getting a little nervous. But I am pleased to be able to feel and experience personally all the details that my state of pregnancy involves.

I notice that almost to the end of the fourth month there is no sign of a bump. There is no need to dress up like a doll. Unless you begin to eat for two you won't put on weight and if you avoid giving in to your whims you might even lose a pound or two. All my clothes fit, apart from those with a tight waist. The clothes seem to squeeze a little but that's because I am more sensitive. I am now woken up at night by cramps in the calves of my legs. I also have contractions of the womb; this seems to happen when I am tired and when I overdo it with the stomach muscles.

However, overall I am fine and I am happy. Since the bump became apparent John has taken over as director of operations: 'When is your next appointment with the doctor? Did you take your medicine?' He now takes an active part in everything.

When I cry out in my sleep he wakes up, brings me back to reality and calms me. 'Is it cramp? In which leg?' He massages the leg. The cramp disappears; I am calm and reassured.

I examine my breast. Now if I squeeze the nipple something comes out. It is not milk yet; it is cholostrum. I am in my fifth month and when John and I make love we have to invent new ways so as not to disturb our little Poppet.

For over a week now the baby's movements have been more lively and I feel them more and more clearly.

10 October

I finally phoned the gynaecologist to tell him about the contractions. He said that they have to be stopped. Total rest. He prescribed medicine to relax the muscles and, if the contractions do not stop, an antispasmodic.

22 October

Appointment with the gynaecologist. I arrived panting and out of breath. I went on the bus and I found myself pushed on all sides by rowdy youngsters of the scarves and banners type. There was an important match on at the stadium. I had to put myself directly in the eye of the storm! To survive at all I have to get off two stops before the clinic. Because of this I was late and had to run all the way to the doctor's consulting rooms to be on time for my appointment.

John was waiting for me at the entrance to the clinic and when he saw me so bedraggled he gave me a bit of a telling off for my behaviour. We went up. I seemed all right to look at. Then came the examination. The gynaecologist was short and sweet. In warning tones he said: 'Madam, if you do not go to bed now, you will give birth this evening. The mouth of the womb is already enlarged, two fingers wide. The head is already in position. Don't you realise that you are having contractions?'

Yes indeed, I was aware of this. But I had tried to play down their importance. I was being over-confident and I was doing the wrong thing.

'Go home at once and go to bed. On the way get yourself an antispasmodic injection and have it administered. Otherwise you will not make it. When you get home begin the muscle relaxant treatment: an injection every three hours, night and day, absolute rest in bed until the end, which, hopefully, will be as long away as possible!'

This was the sentence that every woman fears, 'Stay in bed'. I too feared it. Now it was my turn. But at that moment I was so afraid that even this sentence seemed to me, as it was in fact, my hope of being saved. Anything that I could possibly do, I would have done.

I still had not begun my seventh month. The gynaecologist added: 'Ring me whatever happens, at any hour of the day or night. If labour begins don't waste any time; don't come to the clinic. We will have to go to a hospital where they are equipped to deal with premature babies. Call me.'

'If he were to be born today', I said in a trembling voice 'what chances has he of survival?' 'Madam, it is pointless for me to say that if he were to be born this evening he would have virtually no chance'.

John and I left with a weight on our hearts. We were afraid of what might happen and yet willing to do anything to save Poppet. John drove as if he were transporting dynamite. I was lying on the back seat looking out at the sky and unable even to cry. Is it possible that it will all end like this, in a bursting bubble?

There are those whose children kill them. Yet others swear that they will never have any children. We wanted you and now we risk losing you. I wanted you. John too wanted you. I saw that now in the disappointment and worry written all over his face. He had perhaps never given any thought to the possibility that you wouldn't survive and now he suddenly realised how attached he had become to you.

I wanted you. Yet I had not prayed to God to save you. It seemed that I would be asking too much. If that is how it has to be, then so be it. But Lord, grant that if I do lose this child the loss will not become the centre of my life. I do not want to be like those women, those people who go on suffering a loss, spend the rest of their lives talking about it, tormenting themselves and others with their endless, painful and useless litany of woes. I do not want to end up like that.

I do not want to live beside John like a ghost, a spectre, or, worse still, become a burden on him. I would like, after the initial shock, to retain a clear view of things and look to the future. Life does not end at thirty because of a miscarriage. It cannot be so.

Thus my last day of freedom disappears. Your days of carefree gadding about in my womb are over. Three and a half long months in bed lie ahead of me; three and a half months of solitude and worry on your behalf. So be it. If these months are the answer I will remain calm and quiet, quiet, quiet, for whatever period is necessary. I would stay in bed until the end of my days for you. But you must hang on too, Poppet. Don't play any tricks; you're still too small to be born!

23 *October*

The night has passed and we are still together. John and I look at each other with some misgivings. It would appear that the worst is over. But one never knows. The contractions can always begin all over again. We begin to count the days. Every day that passes is already a day gained. You will grow a little more and the risks will diminish, however slightly. I have decided not to write any more and not to say any more about you until you are out of danger.

30 October

Please Poppet, don't die, be born. I am not sure if I want you to be born just to mark a kind of personal achievement or to be sure of having a baby in the near future. Or perhaps it is out of love for you, real love for you who have already become so dear to me. All three motives together; all three mixed together and all important.

Since you have been there inside me one thing has become crystal clear to me: my desire to have a baby. Even to have another baby apart from you, as well as you, naturally, even though if we were to lose you I would be filled with a sense of loneliness.

That kind of love which is willing to make sacrifices for children is now being made clear to me: it is all-embracing and very specific, very personal, different for each child and, even if limited, as strong as possible for each one.

Anyway, you just try to be born. Don't be upset by my carelessness, by my brusque way of doing things, by me. I am not that bad after all.

Everything is ready for you. Whether you are a boy or a girl there is room for you in our home, in our world, in our hearts. Were you to die you would leave an enormous void.

Whether you are a boy or a girl, healthy or not too robust, destined for great things or even for a simple, ordinary existence, whether you are going to be good or not (your parents will overlook a lot of mistakes), we already love you so much and think only of you. You just think of being born.

10 November

Sometimes I wonder if it is right to want you at any cost. Perhaps it is not by chance that things are not working out so well. Perhaps those early contractions were in fact meant to get rid of a deformed foetus. Perhaps it was all a mistake. Better that you should die.

Should I get up and stop all the medication? I do not know. But I do know that I cannot help you to die. Whatever your state of health I am utterly convinced that I must do all in my power to help you to live.

1983

3 January

Through God's will we have reached the month of January. It is a while since I wrote anything. What was there to say?

First there was fear; then uneasiness and then boredom. Now there is hope, a degree of calm but still a feeling of fatigue.

I had hoped that we might gain a few days at the end but now the final crusts are a bit hard to chew. I find the going a bit heavy.

It seems incredible that I will have a baby. When I think about it, so many people have babies in the normal way, but perhaps the strength of my desire and these present difficulties make the whole process unreal for me.

Will that joy that we are now anticipating be realised? How will I feel after the birth? I am afraid that at the last minute something unforeseen will somehow diminish that great emotional moment and that after so many months in bed I will have no energy for anything when it is all over.

I am overcome by anxiety but John consoles me in my uncertainty. Everything comes and everything passes. In a short time now, one way or another it will all be over. I fell into my husband's arms and gripped his unexpectedly strong shoulders.

I thank God for the warmth of John's love, for his help and protection, for his reassurance and the clarity that his words bring to my life, for the hope and consolation, and for all those things that we will live out together in the future.

25 January

O Lord, long may John be with me! My heart is filled with emotion when I contemplate the great love which we have for each other today. I look on him with tenderness as he faces up to his difficult daily chores with a determination and sense of sacrifice that are unknown to me. It hurts me to see my young man not being loved enough. He lives for me, for us, without ever asking for anything.

I hope our baby will love John. I will teach him to love him.

I have learned to count on John; this young man will be a source of strength to our baby; he is a worker who keeps to himself; deep down, a simple man.

I would like to love him and understand him more than I am capable of today. I should love him to find in me and in our baby that warmth he so seldom finds outside the home. Today, even though in the past I have despised John and have had hateful and hurtful arguments with him, I hope that baby will be like him, a much more positive person than I am.

4 February

Yesterday you were born. John was right. It is useless, stupid and counterproductive to worry about what will happen in the future. We should reserve our best energies for what is happening now. Above all, and this is my view, reality is often so different, so much better than how we imagined it would be. I was afraid that you would be ill. But you are healthy and strong. I was afraid for myself but I, too, am alive.

I was scared at the thought of the effects that pain would have on me: what would become of me? I did not wish to see myself or to appear to others as dishevelled and ugly. I wanted my movements to be measured and graceful, I wanted to appear beautiful, not to destroy the charm and solemnity of the moment. I suffered less pain than I had expected, even though I must admit that it was the worst pain that I had ever experienced. I was worried that it would go on for ages but in the end it wasn't as bad as I had feared.

Everything was different from what I had foreseen. Far from being premature! The time was up, nothing happened. We hung on for the so-called 'obstetric week'! Still nothing. Patience for another few days. Still nothing. The gynaecologist had said that if nothing happened by the third day I would have to be taken into hospital. 3 February dawned.

Despite the sleeping tablet I had slept very badly. Perhaps Poppet will be born tomorrow! At 8.00 punctually I arrived at the hospital reception. John was carrying my suitcase — your things are in it too. I felt important as I prepared the suitcase for both of us. There was none of the sadness about the packing this time, unlike the day when John did the packing in my moment of danger.

I was not sure that you would be born on that day. We

had become used to waiting. It seemed impossible that anything would happen. I was now amazed that the things I had prepared for you would finally be used. I could not even bear to look at them when there was a danger of losing you. Now they are no longer just the subject of dreams.

At 8.30 I am in the bed that is to become my bed of labour. John is there with the gynaecologist and a nurse. At 8.45 they attach the drip.

It is now 9.00 and the contractions begin. Suddenly they are strong and very close together. At 10.00 my mother arrives. I had thought I would not have wanted her to be present, but now that she is here I am happy. She has gone through all of this and yet she is nervous. Her daughter is about to give birth. Her daughter is finally a woman. Her own child has finally grown up. She knows that with the arrival of a baby life begins in earnest.

It is now 11.00. The gynaecologist had said it would be today. Dilation — one centimetre. Patience. The contractions follow each other in rapid succession — strong and ever more frequent. Oh! the pain! Yet it is all so beautiful. It is my son who is about to be born.

He struggles against my womb. Perhaps he does not want to leave the dark heat where he has nestled for so many months. We get on well together.

I felt so close to everyone. So many signs of affection and genuine human warmth, so much unexpected friendship. But between myself and my baby there is a special friendship. There is an intimacy and love of a kind that could not be foreseen.

This relationship is about to be broken. Another contraction. I do not want to shout or cry out, I do not want to let myself go. I cry softly. Mother looks at me. She feels I am suffering. She mops my brow. 'You'll be all right'. With her caressing hand she wants to save me from all of life's ugliness.

40

But I am not unhappy: I am crying to vent my feelings. I feel calm, contented. You are about to arrive. With every push you are nearer. Another contraction, what about my breathing? I had better do what I had been practising. 'Relax, breathe in.' Feel the air entering. The lungs expand. Now they are full. Feel the air going out through your mouth. Now it is all out. Relax your foot; it is hot, it feels heavy. It is relaxed. Breathe....

Relax your leg, it is hot, it feels heavy. It is relaxed. Breathe... it works. I breathe, and my body with all its pain feels as if it does not belong to me any more. That's better. Now I can think right through my labour. Every now and then they come and examine me. Dilation at three centimetres but not advancing. There is some talk of a caesarean.... O God! hopefully not! I do not want to be put to sleep. I want to be conscious when my son is born. I would be unhappy if it had to come to a caesarean. I would be disappointed not to go to the very end as others do. I am angry with myself, with my womb that is making me feel so inadequate. Another contraction.

John comes and goes. Mother remains outside. The room is darkened and there is silence. What peace, what calm. I am so fortunate. I have a room all to myself with a nice view of the Roman countryside. I am comfortable here. I will eat well and will be able to sleep. We can afford this. There are many who cannot.

How much worse to give birth in noisy confusion in miserable hospital surroundings. I have brought a few nice dresses for myself and lovely little baby clothes for you. If we need any more we'll buy them. Again I can afford this and again there are many who cannot. You are lucky. Another contraction.

John is beside me. He holds my hand. He knows how to be near me without intruding. He would love to be able to do more. He paces up and down like a lion in a cage when

41

he is outside the room. I tell him how grateful I am for his presence, for his discretion and for his valuable help, for the love that he is showing for us, for you. Another contraction. It is 4.00. 'Madam, I feel we should go for the caesarean before there is any weakening of the heartbeat. Do you not agree?' 'Yes, you are right.' We disagree about an anaesthetic. My son born while I am asleep? No, I do not want to be asleep. I want to see. I choose an epidural. They bring along a trolley and I am placed on it. I am resigned. At one and the same time I experience fear and confidence. Determination wins out: one way or another you have to be born. Another contraction.

I enter the operating theatre. The anaesthetist arrives to give me the epidural. Without warning I begin to cry. I am in a state of total terror.

I have lost confidence in him. Will he be able to give the injection properly? He inserts the needle in my back. I just sob and sob. I try to steady myself, to remain immobile. Another contraction. He gets angry because I am moving. He shouts at me. He slaps me with his open hand 'Stay still!' I try again.

Again he inserts the needle. From the feet upwards as far as the breast I feel an enormous sensation of warmth. I have no feeling now. I touch myself and feel nothing. Will I feel pain?

Another contraction. It is true. I feel no pain. First a horizontal cut and then a vertical one. You are about to be born.

There you are, out at last! In a moment you will cry out your greeting to life. You do cry out. You are alive!

What a feeling. I laugh and cry simultaneously. I am so happy. Let me see you! You are so beautiful. Maybe you just seem beautiful to me. I know your chin is a bit twisted, your little face a bit creased and your nose squashed after being so long in such a cramped space. I ask: 'But is he ugly?' 'Such a beautiful child, he must be all of ten pounds and you ask if he is ugly!' Even if he was ugly it would not matter to me in the slightest. Indeed, you might even be better off if you were not too good-looking. Then you would have to develop other qualities in order to please people. I put my hand out to touch you, to place it on you, to be the first to caress you. You are all damp. You cry out with a fine strong cry. In return for my caress, there you are with your head down, being held by one leg, and you show your first sign of disrespect for your mother by peeing all over me.

5 February

God has heard my prayer. He knew how much I wanted to breastfeed you and already I have a good supply of milk. You may have a lot of things to learn in life but sucking is not one of them. That you know how to do with a vengeance.

So much vitality in such a small bundle is absolutely amazing. Perhaps you attack so wholeheartedly because you realise that your survival depends on this thick, sticky, tepid liquid. It is an instinct, and such a strong one. It is a sign of your will to live.

I had always believed that you would really take it out on me when breastfeeding but I am so happy that I can afford to be generous.

I put the idea to John as if it were my own: 'Will we call him David?' David is the name that he really wanted. I am feeding you again and seeing you in the flesh after depending for so long on my imagination. Are these the feet that kicked me? They are so small — is it possible? These are the little hands that you sucked, this is the face that for so long I just dreamt about. I gaze at you and realise that while I love you, for the moment you are a perfect stranger, no longer a foetus but a child. We have to get to know each other. It will take some time. Will you like me? I hope so. Already you have changed so much in me and in John and in our family, just by being here with us. I feel that you, my baby, are destined for great things. But where did I hear that before? It's what every mother says about her child!

10 February

I have been here now for seven days. The doctor came and examined me. He looked at the wound and took out the remaining stitches. He told me that if it was all right with the paediatrician I could go home. Home. We are going home. Now there are three of us. I cannot wait for the time when I will really be taking care of you. Up to now it was almost a game: you came to be fed; you stayed a while in my arms or in John's or lying comfortably in your cot. Just a few minutes. You were brought in changed and washed and rested. It was almost a courtesy call. I have no idea whether you sleep at night or cry and I know nothing of your habits; the difficulties involved in minding a small baby are really a closed book to me.

I never had anything to do with children; you are my first child and, medical theory apart, I know nothing about rearing children. And yet I know I will be able to devote myself to you; in fact I feel I am the person best equipped for the job. Even though our relationship is just beginning and the links between us are still somewhat tenuous, I know that I am the most qualified person, the only one with any right to make decisions on your behalf. Mine must be the last word where you are concerned. I want to go home to be able to do things my own way. I want to be able to see you when I want to and not just according to a schedule. I want to treat you like my son and not just like a sterile object. I want to play with you, joke with you and enjoy your company.

I have put our things together. I look at myself in the mirror: the maternity dress is empty looking and the face is no longer that of the young girl of last week. I have changed so much inside and out. My face is pale and I have got thin. I weigh less than before I was expecting you. But in the dark circled eyes there is a look of determination: I feel very strong, stronger than before. No task would be too much for me. Perhaps it is pride, but the fact that I have successfully given birth to you has given me a sense of importance. Let's go. I say goodbye to everyone and they all say goodbye to you with great affection.

John has come to collect us. He looks at us. Now there is me and him and you. The relationship that existed between us at the beginning of this adventure is gone by the board. His ambiguous attitude to me and to my bulging tummy has changed completely. Everything is different. We are now dealing with a different reality. We have to somehow start all over again. John sighs. He gives me the suitcase and he takes you in his arms. From the way he is looking at you I gather that he is full of good will towards you. John was always a good driver. But today the car hooters are blowing behind us exasperatedly. Even when we keep to our own side of the road we seem to be interfering. He doesn't dare either to brake or accelerate.

We have to try to understand him. This is the first time for him to have you in the car. He will become accustomed to having you in the back seat. We returned by the same route as we had travelled to the hospital a week ago. The road was the same but what a change of atmosphere!

We must hurry up and get home because you need to be fed again soon. We stopped briefly and hurriedly at the pharmacy...we needed to buy a thousand things for you and then we stopped at the bakery to buy a cake for ourselves. The cake was obligatory; it is after all a festive occasion.

God only knows how long I will continue to be amazed at having you here. I entered the bedroom absentmindedly. The red of your carry cot, contrasting as it did with the white of the bedspread, took me by surprise. Everything is quiet. You are asleep. Now it is different than when I alone inhabited the house. When I stopped everything stopped. Now it is different. Your presence will fill this room with surprise sounds day and night. The present quiet is just a pause. Piles of clothes and boxes of nappies and the innumerable gadgets judged indispensable have already filled every corner. You will fill every corner of my life as I respond to the rhythm of your feeding times. Even if I were tempted to be sad and waste my time in useless boredom you will not give me the opportunity.

15 February

It reminds me of getting a present of a bicycle as a child. You dream about it, you envy other children their bicycles and you write to Santa Claus. Now you have one. The joy of it all makes you forget everything else. You show it to everyone and, as soon as you can, you get on it enthusiastically and you spend all your free time with it. But still you are not able to ride it properly. It is a problem getting on; the saddle is a bit too high; it is difficult to keep your balance and to apply the brakes gently so that a sudden stop doesn't bring you crashing to the ground. You need time and practice.

For a while every movement requires concentration and a certain amount of time. If you want to ring the bell you have to look to see where it is and you take your eyes off the road. You have to take one hand off the handlebar and hold on with the other and finally push the bell without making the bicycle swerve. But you learn very quickly. Soon the action becomes automatic and requires no particular concentration.

I will learn to change a nappy, dress you, feed you and give you a bath. These will become so much second nature to me that I will be able to laugh at the difficulties I am now experiencing. But for the moment there is nothing to laugh at. Just getting through these essentials is for the moment extremely heavy going. There is no time for anything else. I do feel a need to be able to get back to doing things as I did previously. I must find a way of making the bed, doing the shopping, cleaning the house and providing something more substantial than a quick fry for our meals. Then I must find time to go for a walk, to chat with a friend, buy myself a new dress, even sit down quietly and read without having the feeling that something needs to be dealt with urgently. At the moment all this is a mirage. Little by little!

I have decided that each day, as I get quicker at dealing with you, I will do one of the activities that I used to do before. Today we will do the shopping. What an undertaking! The pram doesn't fit in the lift. So I had to cart it down the stairs. It isn't all that easy to push a pram in a straight line, to make it go where you want it to go. Never before was I so conscious of steps and of the number of obstacles to be avoided between here and the shops. The crossing signals seemed unusually short today. You noticed nothing or else you took it all philosophically in your stride. You just sleep snugly and couldn't care less.

16 February

When I came back today I noticed something that I had forgotten about. Hanging at the entrance of the apartment block was the little blue rosette which I had prepared under pressure. John had hung it there when you were born and it was still there, fluttering.* At the outset I thought it was a sign of weakness, a bit of an outmoded custom, but when I saw it in the lobby today I felt a certain sympathy towards the idea. It works as far as other people are concerned. Even the precise old man on the fourth floor who, when you salute him, touches the rim of his hat and shows the merest crack of a smile on the corner of his mouth and moves off staring into the middle distance; even he, when we met him coming out of the lift said: 'Oh, this is the newborn baby. Let's see him. Congratulations!'

I no longer think it is such a stupid custom. In fact it is a very simple and human way to announce a birth. I am glad I gave in to the pressure. It took you to make me do the kind of things that other people do, without being too complicated, too critical and too rigid in my views. I used to be too proud and lacked simplicity and wisdom.

---

* An Italian custom.

24 February

The alarm rings. It is midnight. It is time for you to be fed. I hesitate before getting up. I am slow to leave the warm comfort of the blankets. Getting up is troublesome. Just another minute... I am going... I must go. John gives a shout. Half awake and half asleep he urges me to get up. Anyway you were in full voice at 2.00 in the morning. No trouble in waking up. A quick look at John and an equally quick flash of envy. I pick my way carefully through the darkness in order not to wake him and go into your room.

We will get through it quickly. Luckily I do not have to worry about bottles and teats at this hour of the night. I give you my own milk. It is dead easy. I just offer you my breast. You know well what you have to do, you take it in your mouth and suck away for all you are worth. Your cot is in a corner of the sitting room. During the day you are in our room but at night we put you here. I would like to have kept you beside me even at night. I might even have considered putting you in the bed beside us but John would not have it. Our bed is his stronghold and he defends it even against an invasion by you. 'It's all right during the day, but please, at night, not here....' I know he is right. Though I do it willingly, it is tiring dealing with you and we do need a break. The interruption is good for the mind. The confines of the bed must remain our territory and if there is any attempt on my part to breach the rules John soon reminds me that I am his wife as well as your mother. I am so taken up with you that I am neglecting him.

At the outset I was delighted with my new-found agility once I no longer had the bulge, and I really made up for lost time. But once again I find that I am no longer mistress of my own body. Again I am carrying you, cradling you, reassuring you and acting as your feeding station. These thoughts are going through my mind as I watch you sleep peacefully. I hate waking you: I touch your cheek ever so gently, I call you, again, ever so gently and then I pick you up carefully. I feel a bit chilly and it is pleasant to hold such a soft warm little bundle in my arms.

I must tell you this: now that I am here I am going to enjoy this experience. While you are feeding I begin to think and I dwell on those thoughts which during the day I could not allow to develop. There are those who speak of the ecstacy of breastfeeding; they talk in hushed tones about voluptuous sensations and unheard of pleasures. I have not felt any of these things. However, I do feel a great sense of peace sitting here on the sofa with you nestling in my arms.

I am doing something for you which I feel is beneficial. You will flatten my breasts... but what about it... I was never a Brigitte Bardot! You suck, you take a rest; then you suck again and finally you have enough. Now I will change you and put you back to bed. You smile, you kick up your feet, you gurgle. You invite me to play with you but I have to pay for it in milk.

It amuses me to watch you all wrapped up in your tiny clothes — tiny, and yet they seem to be too big for you. I hold on to you for a while and rock you in my arms. But all to no avail; your breathing becomes regular and you are asleep already. I cover you up again and fix the cot — now these things have become automatic — and I go back to our room slowly.

30 March

'That doesn't do the child any good.'
'That will harm the baby.'
'Do it for the baby's sake.'
'You can't do that, think of the baby.'
And what about me? Do I count for nothing? He has been here for such a short time and already he is more important than me. Now I am just the mother of my son. It would appear that that is my only importance. Do I count at all in my own right?

If I am to live in peace I have to stop arguing and stop feeling like a fish thrashing to and fro looking for a way out of the net in which it is caught. I have what I always wanted to have. I am John's wife and David's mother and I always knew that it would be difficult. But over and above the difficulty, indeed, as well as the difficulty, life is also pleasant. I have to decide to play my part without intolerance and stupid recriminations. If you are to be happy a time will come when your self-interest must take a back seat. You will have to be willing to 'lose yourself'. This may well be the price that has to be paid for holding on to what is important. When you achieve this, life does reward you and many other things come as a bonus.

The fact is that I have to become like that vast number of women who live in a state of self-forgetfulness. Their aim in life is to help other people, which they do joyfully and not out of resignation. If only I were less childish and egotistical I would understand how all this fits into place; it is right and just, almost the natural order of things.

Such women are indispensable. What would the world be, I mean the world of men, were it not for that band of women who daily care for men and things? And what indeed would become of all those women whose lifestyle resembles that of men? How would they survive if they did not have someone who acted for them as a mother, a wife? Men need someone, a woman, unless they are one of those exceptional men who are not afraid to learn to be involved in those areas traditionally reserved for women. Wife. Mother. You get up a little earlier. You go to bed a little later than the others. Very little time for yourself and the little bit you have is stolen from something else.

How, then, should I live? What is the motivation? Will I be happy? Love is your life source, but that same love will also be your death sentence if it is not appreciated, respected and reciprocated. Seems little enough. But if we do not give the matter some thought our actions can become somewhat meaningless.

When a man takes off a dirty shirt he throws it on a chair. When he wants it later he looks for it in a drawer and finds it there: pleased, he puts it on and buttons it up. It is clean. It is obvious. He does not wonder about the mystery of how it got there for him to put on. Someone picked it up, put it where it should be, washed it without damaging it or shrinking it, ironed it without scorching it and folded it without creases. The loose button has been reanchored! Then it finds its way back into the cupboard, visible and easy to find. After all, it is a favourite shirt!

Caring for others should not be about bustle and noise; it involves a series of small but fundamentally important items. If we are to avoid fatigue and boredom a special kind of love is required. It is the kind of love that transforms a woman into a wife and does not reduce her to a servant. A wife is a mother. There are wives who are mothers willingly and who are happy to live out this reality: they face up to crises, anticipate desires, foresee needs, know what to do when husbands and children have a vague feeling of being ill at ease without knowing exactly what is wrong with them. For all of this you need love. One must ultimately choose a lifestyle that is not geared to self-fulfilment but to fulfilling someone else.

Must I become like that? I do not know if I want to. I do not even know if I can. The truth is that for the moment it is a distant horizon. But I can try.

20 June

At last it is night. During the day I do not know how to divide my time. But this is your final feed. I do not need to hurry your feed and then do the cleaning; hurry your feed and then do the shopping; feed you and then give John his dinner. At night I can feed you calmly. When it is over all I have to do is go to bed. The night is my own and I can arrange my time as I will. I can even spend part of it with you. I have decided that today will be the last time I will wake you for feeding. Four and a half months is long enough on that regime. In any case, I feel a need to repossess myself. You can wake me during the night.

I want to begin to eat what I feel like again; I might even go on a diet and lose a bit of weight; I want to dress the way I would like to, in a nice dress closed at the back and not a button in sight on the front. I want to feel free not to wash for an entire day. But none of this is possible if you are hanging off me all the time. I had decided. But now that it has come to the last time I feel a sense of regret.

Our nightly meetings have an aura of poetic wistfulness and tenderness. Being close to each other in the night, lingering together so that I could give you that extra hug and kiss without feeling like a child stealing jam, creates its own intimate atmosphere of complicity which I know I will miss. There we were alone, you sleeping peacefully in my arms while I listened to your breathing and to the noises from the street. All right, we will go on for one more day and I will stop tomorrow.

3 August

I put you into the little carrier seat that I had attached to my bicycle. You were excited at the novelty of it all but you were very quickly at home in your new seat, holding on tightly and studying the world from a new vantage point. This is our first trip together on my bicycle. You are happy, very pleased indeed. Not a sign of fear; you trust me implicitly, blindly; I am the mother, your source of all goodness and truth. I will take it easy; nevertheless I am a little impatient. I want to show you all the lovely places that are in store for you. I start to pedal towards the beach. You look around and all the neighbours look at you. Those that know you say 'Isn't he lovely! What a beautiful little baby!' Others just smile, feeling a sense of gentleness at the sight of us. And off I go, proud of my charge. I continue to pedal towards the tower, the wind in my hair, the sun on my back, enjoying the familiar colours of the sky, the sand and the trees.

You look around with great curiosity. You point to things that seem to interest you. You seem to want to say: 'Let's go over there; let's go down that way'. Certainly, we will go wherever you please. I am enjoying the sensation of doing what I really want to do, but now it is not in spite of you, or despite the fact that I have you, but in your company.

1 September

Perhaps one day I will be sufficiently forgetful to trot out the same story as many others do, that it was terrible giving up work, that I made the sacrifice for you. But I hope this will not happen. I hope I will not forget the real truth. I am happy and pleased to be your mother and it gives me greater satisfaction to continue to be your mother than to be 'fulfilled' in a career outside the home.

Maybe I will eventually regret the decision but I must face up to that. I must also face up to John's disapproval and, into the bargain, run the gauntlet of the smug remarks of all those who say that I just gave up. Anyway. Today I missed the train that was destined to carry me on to a brilliant career as a doctor and I have taken up a more modest position beside your cot. Perhaps another train will come along later, perhaps never. But I have missed this one forever.

Now that I have decided, now that the doubts have disappeared, now that I have you in my arms and your baggage around me, I feel a sense of liberation and freedom. I will do what I want to do and today I want to remain with you. I do not want to give my earnings to someone else who would rear you on my behalf. I do not want to go out, no matter where, and be thinking only of you. It should not be someone else who answers when in fact it is me you want. In the end you would not want me anymore. I do not want to be elsewhere when you laugh for the first time, when you say your first word, when you let go of the chair and take your first steps and throw yourself into waiting arms. I want it to be into my arms. I want to be there. I want to witness all the little faces that you pull; there are some little faces that happen only once. I want to see those ones; I never want to forget them.

So, today I have chosen to stay at home, at least for a year, to be with you. I am fortunate to be able to do this. I may well forget what my motives were, be unfaithful to myself and whinge about my decision in the future. But today this is what I want. This is my desire, it is a need, a necessity for me and not only for you.

6 October

Today I gave you a haircut. This is the first time. It changed your face. The loss of three curly locks makes all the difference. You are no longer yourself, no longer an infant; you are a baby now. The three locks of hair are on the table and I haven't got the courage to throw them out.

What is happening to me? Am I going soft and sentimental? I need a bit more realism; what I am now contemplating doing is what I have always disapproved of, derided and scoffed at when others were doing it. But this is what I want. I take the fine, almost blond hairs between my fingers, tie them with a little ribbon just as my grandmother did for her children, just as my mother did, and I put them in the top drawer of the dressing table.

1984

15 January

My friend Susan rang me this morning. She is pregnant again just a few months after the birth of her first child. She was still in a state of uncertainty but very conscious of what this would mean for her. She kept repeating this to me, trying to convince me and herself, but the overtones of joy in her voice were obvious. I knew she was happy.

In a way I envied her. My child is still smaller than hers — I was overcome by a wave of tenderness. I would have liked to be in her position. Today I mentioned this to a colleague and she looked at me with dismay and disbelief. She looked at me, wide-eyed, as if I had uttered an indecency and she exclaimed: 'But seriously, would you really like that? Another son? Why?' 'Because I would like to.' I see disapproval, disdain, almost, in her every look. I seem to her to be incorrigible. I insist that I will persist in this folly. I must be mad: I married before finishing my studies. It does not matter that I had known John for six years before we married and that I finished my studies anyway. I began my work as a doctor and, better again, I became pregnant. She is not interested in hearing that it was not an accident, that it all transpired because I wanted it that way. When she heard that I wanted to go through all that again her esteem for me was shaken. Evidently, I do not want to improve my situation. It really hurts her. I do not make any pretence that she understands me. She has no children, she is not even married; she does not even have a boyfriend. She thinks only of her work and she reaps the benefits.

In that area she has all the things that I will never have but on the other hand she lacks what I acquired so hastily from life. Neither of us is wrong. In life everyone is different.

Different people have different values. For me, having children is what counts more than anything else.

Should I feel guilty if this is what attracts me? Do I owe an explanation to all those who feel that this is yet another step towards total dissolution? What answer can I give to those who judge me to be indulging unreasonable desires? It is not easy to justify. The idea of a child, another child, now seems to attract me irresistibly.

It is not a case of wanting to play with dolls. I now know what is at stake. I could produce a thousand reasons: for example I could suggest you might need company. But this is not true. I was an only child and there were no problems. Or again I could say that I would like to have a little girl but that wouldn't be true either. Who knows whether it would be a boy or a girl? In fact, when I think about it I feel, for no good reason, that it would be another little boy.

Another reason might be that I want to give myself a reason for not being back at work, at least not yet. This is perhaps not totally absurd. On some occasions I have considered a child as a means of not facing up to the fear of beginning again, now that I am out of the mainstream. Remain at home. Keep the problem at a safe distance. But even this in a way created a new problem. But it is not like that today. Why then?

Because this is what I really want. That is the sole reason. Because I want to live that adventure which is the bringing up of a human being. Every new child is a new adventure because with every child a new and unique relationship is created. I have not been the same since you were born and every newborn is totally different. Thus, just as there are a thousand ways of expressing love, and just as each man's feelings towards you are different, so, too, I believe there are a thousand different ways of being a mother.

I would like to know what you would think. The idea of meeting another child as I meet you every day fascinates me. How would he look, this new and unforeseeable fruit of my union with John? Another temperament, a different way of looking at life, other ideas in his head, another destiny. What stimulates me is this idea of diversity. I feel challenged to solve the problems that will arise and which in your case were easy enough. What moves me is the desire for another unique being, the desire to know him and understand all his personal characteristics. Once again I would like to undertake the difficult but exciting task of bringing him up, of developing all his capabilities, of discovering and promoting all his gifts, of seeking out his talents together with John and you, of helping him to reach his full potential.

I would like to offer him the entire world for his enjoyment as I offer it to you. I would like the entire world to rejoice in him and listen to what he has to offer. In a word, I would like to love him. In fact, while I await his birth at a remote future date, or never, I already love him just as I loved you before you were born. Grant that the miracle may happen again. Who knows, even after him I may not be satisfied, I may not have enough....

28 March

'Once upon a time, far far away in a distant land — and who knows but it may still exist — there was a huge blue sea. Over it was a blue sky flecked with thick white clouds. In the daytime they were not visible but at night millions of bright stars shone out. They sat there, side by side, chatting to each other. They were all very bright but one in particular, small and very good, shone brighter than all the rest. What will we call it? How about Twinkle?' 'Yes, yes!' Now I have to invent fairy stories and sing. I have unearthed poetic and musical talents which I never thought I had. All this, just to get you to sleep.

Twinkle, the adventurous little star, has come to my rescue night after night. Come on, go to sleep now. Please. Sleep, sleep. Then I will sleep too.

10 July

You are sick, so sick that you are not even able to cry. You settled into the bed in the hospital, your forehead burning, your cheeks red and your feverish eyes closed. You hold on to my finger in your hand; when I move you open your eyes for an instant, tighten your grip, then loosen it again as if you did not have the strength to hold on for long. Don't worry, I'm going nowhere; I won't go away. Where could I go with you so sick? I hang on to the doctor's every word and I ask him outlandish questions, almost forgetting that I am a doctor myself.

He answers patiently: he is used to mothers and to doctors who, when the patient is a member of their own family, seem to act stupidly. He goes away and time passes slowly and boringly, punctuated by the most trivial events: a door opens, a window bangs, the thermometer is inserted, the thermometer is withdrawn.

Have we been here for days or is it just hours? The heavy window shades keep the heat at bay. The noises at this time of day are accentuated: the rattle of plates, footsteps coming and going, a canary singing in his cage beneath our window.

Before you were born, I prayed to God that if you were to die my life would not come to a standstill, that I would be able to press ahead regardless. A different love, a different life, a re-examination of myself and the world, an effort to understand life. But luckily you were born.

Now that I know you, now that we have become friends, this is my prayer once again. But it is hard to believe that life would be possible for me. How could I ever live without you? Once deprived, deprived for ever. Please get better! Luckily, you do get better.

1985

15 March

It is spring again. The long winter is well over and now we are back at the seaside for a whole day. The gate creaked when we opened it since it has been closed for so many months. The garden looks abandoned and full of dead leaves. But there is a profusion of flowers, stubborn flowers which, in spite of our neglect, succeed in growing anyway. You look around you as we drive up the short avenue and as soon as the car door is open you are off to explore things.

We open the house to let in some light and get rid of the dampness. Sunlight will soon make it more hospitable. You run from one room to another, touching everything. I shout out: 'Don't touch it; it's all dusty.' Naturally, you ignore me. You want to make things your own by touching them. Now you are out in the garden again. I follow you. The driveway is very uneven and there is a spot at the end where you kept falling last year. Now, even when you run, you hop over that stone time and again and there is no falling. Don't tell me you remember the spot. It is just that now you are really walking, not just waddling; you have grown up and your run is full of confidence.

There you are at the wall which forms the boundary to the larger garden at the back of the house. You stop short, remain on the stile, immobile, and your face lights up and then softens. 'Mamma, 'member?'

Is it possible that you recall the spot? It must be. You are moved to tears, almost like an adult. You look around excitedly. This is where you played, laughed and shouted last year. You go over the stile and take a few cautious steps on the grass. Are you afraid it will disappear? You already have your memories of this house; it is already special for you, as it is for me who saw it being built. I have been here as a child, a teenager and an adult — always happy here.

71

Your reaction pleases me. I too am moved. Perhaps in twenty or thirty years you too will speak with affection of this place: the seaside... my grandparents' house... and your eyes will light up.

20 March

I took you in my arms and stood you on the bed. I must dress you but first of all I look at you. You are beautiful. I give you a hug and a kiss. You like being hugged, you begin to wriggle and to purr but you do not go away from me. I hold you tight and then look at you again. All of a sudden you embrace me and then: 'Mamma, will we get married?'

I am puzzled. What is happening, where would you have heard this? 'I can't marry you, I am already married to Daddy.' 'Come on, Mamma, marry me!' 'But why?' 'Because you are lovely and I really love you.' No doubt you are sincere; I am flattered and overcome. 'I love you too.' More kisses and hugs and simpering.

Mother is still in your dreams, only mother; I am thinking that one day you will repeat all this speech to young girls. It is absurd to feel jealous of your future loves given that you are only a little over two years old! But that is what I feel. All those hussies ready to destroy the precious object of my love!

Am I going crazy, what am I saying? I think I understand what mothers and mothers-in-law feel when their sons discover love. I wonder what my husband's mother thought of me when she learned of my existence. 'Just imagine, a girlfriend. Who is she, what is she like?' Doubts and hesitations about me, a stranger who dared to cast her eyes on a mother's son. 'Will she ever know and understand him, will she ever love him more than his mother who wanted him, bore him, reared him and loved him to this very day?' She never realised that, as far as her son was concerned, I was no longer a stranger, an outsider.

'Will she be able to make him happy?' Yes she will. He knows this. Already, without you knowing it, he nestles

73

his head on her bosom and feels at ease. You have just heard about her but she is already at the centre of all his thoughts, the object of his desires and the source of his happiness. You feel deceived, betrayed by him and tricked by her. You would like to know her, judge her and, after a critical examination, pronounce her worthy of your son. But nobody asks for your opinion. That is how it is and how it should be.

But one thing you can do for him; rather, you could have, for if you have not, it is now too late. You could also do it for her, whoever she may be: love him with a genuine love and teach him to love. If you have done this he will be in a better position to choose, and those best suited to him will choose him. Thus he will enjoy the fullness of love. So, just as he got life from you — which you need not have given — so now he can have happiness or be deprived of it.

20 May

'Look, Mamma, it's lovely!' You take me by the hand and pull me towards the window as I sometimes do to you. 'Look, David, what a wonderful sunset!' It is enough for you that it has become 'lovely', this miracle of the setting sun which we witness evening after evening from our balcony. We live on the top floor. Perhaps because we are most at home in familiar surroundings and perhaps because I was born in a house like this, I am really happy half-way between heaven and earth, with the wind blowing, the rain beating on the windows and the sun scorching hot. Many would not live in an apartment like this on principle: 'It is dangerous and it is hot in the summer and cold in the winter.' Yes, but it is so beautiful. I like to feel myself a victim of the seasons, immersed in the life cycle of the plants and flowers in my pots and boxes as they dry out in summer, shed their leaves in autumn, die in the winter and return to life again in spring. I love this house. I know every inch of it. Everything in it is there because we wanted it and designed it so. You have your room. You play there happily.

The silence, the peace of this road in a quiet, almost isolated village-like atmosphere, the clear sky — these are marvellous advantages. The birds chatter at dusk and their thousand swirling flights will become part of you. Their shrill voices will mark dawn and dusk for all the years that you remain in this house of your childhood. You will never be able to forget them.

At least in your ambitions be like these swallows. Fly high in the heavens, ever more boldly upwards. From up there you will understand how small and insignificant are the things of this earth and that the only thing that matters is the infinite, the eternal.

3 June

Why are we so taken up with this? You have learned in ten days: you pee like Daddy and sit on your little potty. We went together to buy it long before you were ready to use it. 'Which one do you want? — The one in the shape of a car, or a dog or a cat...?'

'The one like a dog!'

You liked it immediately and you began to play with it. You sat astride it like a horse, you put it on your head like a hat, you fed it and gave it drinks as if it were a real dog. Then one day in summer, when I took off your nappy you decided to use it for the purpose for which it was intended. It all happened in ten minutes.

'Look Mamma, I've made a little lake with two little fish in it.' We contemplated this work for a while — you were clapping your hands and I was a bit amazed at your poetic imagination. When calm returned I was about to dump the lot into the toilet then I thought: Hold on, don't throw it away; keep it and show it to Daddy. Why should I deny you full satisfaction? In that way the potty and its contents stayed with us all day. Every now and then I had a look. Finally, that evening, Daddy was home. Before he had time to do anything, and still clutching his brief-case, you dragged him into the toilet. 'Look, Daddy, I made that.' Without quite understanding the situation, he looked. Then he looked at me and looked at you — both of us smiling proudly — and he overcame his distaste and congratulated you.

2 August

You are wearing a pair of slightly oversized boots, a hat on your head and, complete with jumper, you are ready for our expedition to the mountains. This year we have sandwiches for three in our rucksack. Will you be tired? I don't think so. At the speed at which you took off it looked as if you could go to the ends of the earth and back in one day. The hills, the cool breeze, the sun, it's wonderful. How are you taking it? You give me a shiny stone. 'See, Daddy, over there, the snow.' You hold my hand while we are climbing, your stride a little shorter than mine.... 'Sing, Mamma!' I sing a traditional mountain song. Who would have thought that you would be echoing my voice as I sang for you? Today I feel there is nothing lacking in my life. You and me and your father walking in the mountains — so close together and so close to heaven.

1 September

We finally came home after the holidays. The suitcases were still on the landing as I went into the house on my own. I went through the deserted rooms that had taken on that dead atmosphere of not being lived in. It gave me a certain amount of pleasure to be able to recognise the shape of the familiar objects in the half light. In a moment this magic silence will be broken by David's shouts and John's voice. Being back at home was reassuring and I enjoyed the sensation of being surrounded by these solid walls, the peace and the familiarity.

I opened the shutters, opened the windows to let in the air and the light, and the colours of my everyday existence came to life. I realised again how much I like it here and how much I missed all this. The rattle of doors. They are arriving. But why the delay, why the silence, why are you not coming in? I leave the suitcase that I have been unpacking on the floor and go and look. You are at the threshold standing still; you are looking in; what are you waiting for? What is wrong? You take a step and look around you and then with your eyes half closed you throw yourself against the wall, arms and legs spread wide for maximum contact. Then you withdraw your cheek and kiss the wall: 'My lovely little house.'

28 September

With whom other than John could I make love as I did tonight? Passionate abandon and uninhibited spontaneity! Free to receive and free to give without hesitation, unreservedly and without reticence. No need to worry that it would come to an end, intoxicated by the knowledge that it would last forever. Who else could love me as he loves me, as he has loved me to this day, thousands of times? who else would say to me on the following morning while drowning me with kisses. 'Are you really the same person as yesterday? Sensational, sensational!' Tak-tak-tak, the noise of bare feet on the floor. Half asleep you arrive, dummy in your mouth, pillow in your arms, feeling your way in the half light. 'Run, hurry up, come in out of the cold.' You settle in to the reassuring heat of the bed, your eyes still half closed and you enjoy our hugs. 'Let's play cat and kittens, Mamma.' You begin to miaow and to rub against us. Your father begins to miaow with you and pretends to lick you. I begin to purr. And I ask myself, what else could happiness mean?

1 October

'How old are you?'
'Three years in February.'
'Is he very independent?'
Are you independent? Anyway, they have accepted you
and you are enrolled in the playschool. Fortunately or
unfortunately, I do not know which. You have your little
schoolbag and your brand new yellow uniform. I did not
sleep last night. 'Have you got your lunch? And the
handkerchief? Hurry up, we'll be late.'
A stream of mothers, fathers, children and grandparents
up and down the stairs of the school. The classroom is full
of sun and tears, some restrained, some not. The nun takes
you by the hand. A little girl shoves over to make room for
you at the desk and she shows you her drawing. You take
a pencil and a sheet of paper and begin a drawing of your
own. I remain in the corner for a while, looking, but after
a few minutes you have forgotten me and the nun indicates
to me that I should leave. 'Come back in an hour, this is
the first day.' An hour. It could pass quickly or it could be
very long. To pass the time and to prevent me thinking
about it I visit a friend; I end up talking about you.
When I come back you are in the school yard. Where are
you? Over there: 'David.' You turn, look at me and continue
to run about. 'Hallo David, have you no words for me?'
'Hallo Mamma, I'm playing.' Yes, I see. I am disappointed.
Not that I wanted to find you in tears but at least you could
have run to meet me, at least that. Instead you are up and
down on the slide; you run about with the others. In short,
you are enjoying yourself. I am almost offended and I am
ashamed of this sentiment. In the end I have to carry you
bodily away and try to convince you that you can come back
tomorrow. Then we get outside.

'Oh, I forgot, I brought you a present.'

'A present?'

'Yes, look.' You rummage in your schoolbag and then with an air of mystery you show me your closed hand.

'Let me see.'

'There you are.'

'What is it?'

'Can't you see, a little man.'

I do not want to dampen your enthusiasm but I have to explain to you that you cannot take toys from the playschool and bring them home with you. Not even as a present for Mamma.

2 October

Today Daddy took you to school. That way I was able to stay in bed a little longer and enjoy my freedom. I will get a book. I would like to read but I never have the time.... This one...? No... nor this one. I cannot find anything that will interest me.

Perhaps I will do a bit of knitting. I still have a sweater to finish from last year. I do two rows and then I think that it isn't really so urgent. I get up and look at myself in the mirror. I should go to the hairdresser. But not today. Perhaps another day.

What is happening to me? With you at playschool my mornings have become very empty — empty because of your absence and empty of any desire to do anything else. Where has it all led me? The duties and the work I gave up on the pretext that I could not do them because of you, all the other things I wanted to do. Now I feel the way one does after finishing a very difficult examination that for months and months has nailed you to your desk and made you drop all the less essential things from your life. In the end, important things are dropped in favour of study so that only the absolutely indispensable remains. Your whole life is geared towards one goal — to pass the examination. On the day after, this is how you feel: free to do what you want but with the distinct feeling that nothing is worth doing. But I am thinking of you. I am missing you. I have become so used to your presence that now I would almost like to have you back even if it meant constantly giving out to you.

'Be good, come here, stop that....' I will get over it. Yesterday you were playing and singing. I asked you: 'What song is that?' 'Patricia taught it to us.' Who is this Patricia and what is this song that I have never even heard? There is no doubt that you are no longer just mine. I am no longer the only inhabitant of your world. You need my love but I am aware that I also need yours. Undoubtedly, you will change and I am beginning to fear that the intimacy of our relationship will be diminished. Apart from feeding you and minding you I have tried to instil in you the certainty of being loved, self-confidence and enthusiasm for life. I think I have succeeded.

You have become impatient to leave my arms and press on on your own. I know that this is right for you and it is what I want also. But, for my part, this separation is like giving birth to you again and, as it was in the first instance, it is painful now too. You know you can count on me. You will still ask for my help but I have to stop being over-protective. I must allow you to get on with things, trying, failing, learning. I must move into the background and watch you getting on with life.